T0011236

Why Do We Need RAIN?

by Laura K. Murray

PEBBLE
a capstone imprint

Published by Pebble, an imprint of Capstone
1710 Roe Crest Drive, North Mankato, Minnesota 56003

capstonepub.com

Library of Congress Cataloging-in-Publication Data is available on the Library of Congress website.

ISBN: 9780756575434 (hardcover)
ISBN: 9780756575380 (paperback)
ISBN: 9780756575397 (ebook PDF)

Summary: Rainy day got you down? Just remember, rain is necessary to all life on Earth! In this Pebble Explore book, discover how this often overlooked—and sometimes annoying—part of nature is important to our world. We need rain to grow fruits and vegetables and replenish lakes and rivers. Rain is even important to the air we breathe!

Editorial Credits
Editor: Donald Lemke; Designer: Sarah Bennett; Media Researcher: Svetlana Zhurkin; Production Specialist: Katy LaVigne

Image Credits
Dreamstime: Harperdrewart, 21; Getty Images: Andrew Fox, 23, emholk, 28, FatCamera, 19, Martin Paul, 17, Martin Paul, 25, Paul Souders, 22, schulzie, 29 (middle), Willard, 16; Shutterstock: Alexander Demyanov, 29 (bottom), Alf Ribeiro, 4, brgfx, 7, Cozine, 11, Designua, 15, DJTaylor, 20, Faith Forrest (dotted background), cover and throughout, Gorynvd, 18, Humannet (rain background), cover, back cover, and throughout, jantsarik, 8, Jasper Suijten, 26, JJFarq, 9, Juergen Wallstabe, 14, Kekyalyaynen, 24, Liubomyr Tryhubyshyn, 5, Locomotive74, 6, narikin, cover, Pempki, 13, PhilipYb Studio, 29 (top), Shiyari, 12, Toa55, 27

All internet sites appearing in back matter were available and accurate when this book was sent to press.

Printed and bound in the USA. 5425

Table of Contents

Words in **bold** are in the glossary.

Jungle Rain

Clouds hang over the rain forest. Monkeys and birds chatter loudly. Thunder rumbles. Raindrops fall. Rain forests are the rainiest places on Earth. They can get more than 32 feet (9.8 meters) of rain each year.

Humans, animals, and plants need water to live. Rain helps living things get water to drink. It keeps **soil** healthy. It helps plants grow.

People use it in many other ways! Rain is an important part of nature.

All About Rain

Earth's water is found in oceans, rivers, and lakes. Water is stored in the land and soil. It is frozen as snow and ice. It is a gas in the air too.

The Water Cycle

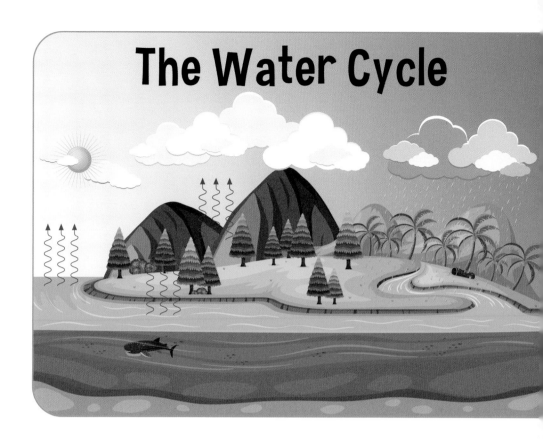

Rain is part of the **water cycle**. The planet's water is always moving. Water from oceans, plants, and other places turns into a gas. It rises into the air. Then it turns back into liquid. It makes clouds. Some clouds become heavy with water. The water falls back to Earth as rain or snow.

Clouds are made up of water in the air. This is called **water vapor**. The clouds also have tiny bits of salt, dust, or smoke. Water vapor grabs onto these tiny bits. A water droplet forms. It bumps into other bits and gets bigger. It becomes a raindrop once it is 0.02 inches (0.5 millimeters). Raindrops can reach up to about 0.25 inches (6 mm) across.

Most water falls from the sky as rain. When the air is cold, water might come down as snow. Other times, it falls as hail or sleet.

People often think raindrops are shaped like tears. But raindrops are all different! Small raindrops may look like jelly beans. Larger raindrops are shaped like hamburger buns. The biggest raindrops flatten as they fall. They break into smaller drops.

Raindrops fall at speeds of 15 to 25 miles (24 to 40 kilometers) per hour. Smaller drops that fall close together are called a drizzle.

The wettest place on Earth is in India. It may get nearly 40 feet (12.2 m) of rain in one year! Most of the rain falls during **monsoon** season. Monsoons are strong winds that come a few times a year. They can bring very wet or very dry weather.

Mumbai, India

The driest place on Earth is Chile's Atacama Desert. It may get less than 2 inches (5 centimeters) of rain all year.

How Does Rain Help Us?

Rain is an important part of the water people use every day. People get freshwater from lakes and rivers. They use water from **reservoirs** and aquifers.

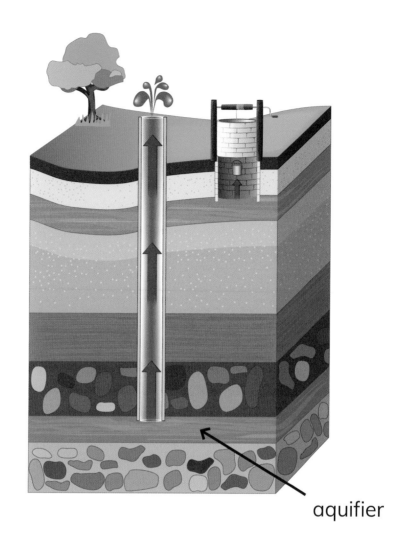

aquifier

Aquifers are underground layers of rocks. They hold water. Then the water flows into wells and springs. Rain helps keep these water storage areas full.

Plants and trees depend on rain. They soak up water from the soil. Then they let out water vapor through their leaves.

Water in the ground also flows into rivers, lakes, and oceans. Sometimes there is too much water to soak up on top of the soil. It becomes runoff. It flows into rivers, lakes, and streams.

Heavy rain can bring flooding. Sudden floods are called flash floods. They are strong enough to destroy buildings, trees, and bridges. They can cause rising water and mudslides.

Rain is important for life on Earth. People use the water for drinking, bathing, and cooking. They use it for washing clothes and dishes. Farmers use it to grow crops and plants. They give water to livestock. Others use water in factories and mines.

People use water to make food, chemicals, paper, and other products. They use it to make electricity too. People also use water for fun. They swim, boat, fish, and surf.

Many people collect rainwater. They may use barrels to catch and store it. Some people use the water on their yards or gardens. Others use it to wash cars or fill swimming pools.

rain garden

Rain gardens are another way to collect rain. Rain gathers in the low areas of land. The area helps rain soak into the soil. Rain gardens help take out pollutants from the water.

Threats to Rain

Today, **climate change** is causing problems in the water cycle. Ice is melting faster. Some places are having more rain and storms than ever. Other places are very dry.

An iceberg melts near Greenland.

Rainwater runoff can be harmful. The water may pick up **fertilizer**, oil, and pollutants. Then the dirty water flows into rivers, lakes, and other places. Sometimes people make this problem worse. They cover the land and forests with roads and buildings. It is harder for the land to soak up water.

Pollution is a big threat to rain. People cause most of the pollution. Harmful gases go into the air. The gases may come from burning coal for electricity. They also come from vehicles and factories.

The gases mix with water and other materials. Polluted rain falls to the earth. It is called acid rain. The acid rain harms plants, wildlife, water, and soil. It can damage buildings too. Acid rain is bad for people's health.

A World Without Rain

Can you imagine a world without rain? Life on Earth would become impossible. There would not be enough fresh water for cooking or bathing. It would be difficult for people to find safe drinking water. Plants, crops, and animals would die.

The water cycle would be destroyed. Water in the soil and air would dry up. **Drought** would be a big problem. Clouds would disappear. The sun would scorch the land. Temps would rise. Wildfires would rage.

Rain is an amazing part of nature. It has an important job in Earth's water cycle. People, animals, plants, and soil depend on rain as nature we need.

COOL FACTS ABOUT RAIN

• Clouds usually look white because of the tiny water droplets inside that reflect sunlight.

• Cloud seeding is when scientists use aircraft or other machines to get clouds to make even more rain.

• People measure rainfall with containers called rain gauges.

• The smell of rain falling on soil is called "petrichor."

• One inch (2.5 cm) of rain falling over one acre (0.4 hectares) is equal to 27,154 gallons (102,789 liters) of water.

• Rain that falls but never reaches the ground is called phantom rain.

Glossary

climate change (KLY-muht CHAYNJ)—a large change in weather patterns

drought (DRAWT)—times of much less rain than normal

fertilizer (fer-tuh-LYE-zuhr)—material added to land to make plants grow

monsoon (muhn-SOON)—a seasonal strong wind that changes directions; it often brings very wet or very dry weather

reservoirs (REZ-er-vwarz)—places where water is collected and stored

soil (SOYL)—the loose material on the surface of the Earth where plants grow; it's made up of tiny particles of rock, organic matter, and other substances.

water cycle (WAH-tuhr SYE-kuhl)—the path of water on, above, and below earth's surface

water vapor (WAH-tuhr VAY-puhr)—the gas form of water

Read More

Gardeski Christina Mia. *All About Rain Forests*. North Mankato, MN: Capstone, 2018.

Rossiter, Brienna. *Rain*. Lake Elmo, MN: Focus Readers, 2020.

Werner, Rachel. *Floods*. North Mankato, MN: Capstone, 2022.

Internet Sites

NASA Climate Kids: What Is the Water Cycle?
climatekids.nasa.gov/water-cycle

US Geological Survey: The Water Cycle
water.usgs.gov/edu/watercycle-kids-beg.html

Weather WizKids: Rain & Floods
https://www.weatherwizkids.com/?page_id=66

Index

About the Author

Laura K. Murray is a Minnesota-based author of more than 100 published or forthcoming books for young readers. She loves learning from fellow readers and helping others find their reading superpowers!
Visit her at LauraKMurray.com.